LOUISE WHITE SCHOOL

DISCARD

PEOPLE OF LONG AGO

Curriculum Consultants

Dr. Arnold L. Willems
Associate Professor of Curriculum and Instruction
The University of Wyoming

Dr. Gerald W. Thompson
Associate Professor
Social Studies Education
Old Dominion University

Dr. Dale Rice
Associate Professor
Department of Elementary and Early Childhood Education
University of South Alabama

Dr. Fred Finley
Assistant Professor of Science Education
University of Wisconsin

Subject Area Consultants

Astronomy
Robert Burnham
Associate Editor
Astronomy Magazine and *Odyssey* Magazine

Geology
Dr. Norman P. Lasca
Professor of Geology
University of Wisconsin — Milwaukee

Oceanography
William MacLeish
Editor
Oceanus Magazine

Paleontology
Linda West
Dinosaur National Monument
Jensen, Utah

Physiology
Kirk Hogan, M.D.
Madison, Wisconsin

Sociology/Anthropology
Dr. Arnold Willems
Associate Professor of Curriculum and Instruction
College of Education
University of Wyoming

Technology
Dr. Robert T. Balmer
Professor of Mechanical Engineering
University of Wisconsin — Milwaukee

Transportation
James A. Knowles
Division of Transportation
Smithsonian Institution

Irving Birnbaum
Air and Space Museum
Smithsonian Institution

Donald Berkebile
Division of Transportation
Smithsonian Institution

Zoology
Dr. Carroll R. Norden
Professor of Zoology
University of Wisconsin —
  Milwaukee

First published in Great Britain by Macmillan Children's
  Books, a division of Macmillan Publishers Ltd, under the
  title *Look It Up.*
First edition copyright © 1979, 1981 Macmillan Publishers Ltd
  (for volumes 1-10)
First edition copyright © 1980, 1981 Macmillan Publishers Ltd
  (for volumes 11-16)
Second edition copyright © 1985, 1986 Macmillan Publishers Ltd

Published in the United States of America

Text this edition copyright © 1986 Raintree Publishers Inc.

Library of Congress Number: 86-562

1 2 3 4 5 6 7 8 9 0   90 89 88 87 86

Printed and bound in the United States of America.

Library of Congress Cataloging-in-Publication Data

Let's discover people of long ago.

  (Let's discover; 7)
  Bibliography: p. 67
  Includes index.
  Summary: A reference book dealing with prehistoric man;
such early civilizations as the Sumerians, Minoans, and
Babylonians; and later societies including the Vikings,
Normans, and Mayas.
  1. Civilization, Ancient—Juvenile literature. 2. Man,
Prehistoric—Juvenile literature. [1. Civilization, Ancient.
2. Man, Prehistoric] I. Title: People of long ago. II. Series.
AG6.L43   vol. 7, 1986   [CB3L]   031s   86-562
ISBN 0-8172-2606-0 (lib. bdg.)
ISBN 0-8172-2587-0 (softcover)

LET'S DISCOVER
PEOPLE OF LONG AGO

RAINTREE PUBLISHERS
Milwaukee

Contents

EARLY MEN AND WOMEN

These people lived 30,000 years ago. Their bones were found in caves in France. They are called Cro-Magnon people. From their bones, we know what they looked like. Cro-Magnon people were shorter than we are, but their brains were the same size.

Cro-Magnons hunted animals for food and made clothes from their skins and sewing needles from their horns.

The discovery of fire

People have used fire for thousands of years. We do not know how they learned to use it. Maybe they discovered it by chance. When two stones are struck together they make a spark. The spark may have set fire to some grass. Below are some ways to make fire.

1

People had seen fires long before they learned how to make fire themselves. They saw lightning start fires.

One way to make fire is to roll a pointed stick into a piece of wood.

4

Another way is to rub a stick up and down a groove in a piece of wood. After a long time, the wood becomes very hot.

Fires made the caves warm and dry. People burned big fires at night to keep wild animals from coming in.

2

In dry, warm weather, trees sometimes caught fire. People became frightened and ran away.

3

Once people learned to make fire, they could cook meat and other foods. They made ovens from small rocks and clay.

5

Wild animals were afraid of fire. These men are using burning sticks to drive off a wild animal.

6

People began farming. They used fire to clear their fields. The ashes left behind made the land good for planting.

The first homes

The earliest people lived in hot parts of the world like Africa. They made their homes in caves. They used caves near lakes or rivers so they would have enough water.

Some caves were long and deep. They were dark inside, so fires were kept burning. The fires made the caves very smoky.

Later people made huts from mud or grass. The animal bones on this round hut make it stronger.

As time went by, people made better huts. Animal skins were placed over wood frames. These huts are like tents.

Some people still live in huts built on wooden frames. The hut below is in modern Papua New Guinea.

Early farming

This is a village in Europe about 3,000 years ago. The people were good farmers. They grew grains and vegetables. They kept cows, pigs, and goats. They built boats and fished.

CRAFTS AND TOOLS

The first tools people used were probably sticks, bones, and stones. Later, people found they could use one flint or stone to chip another one. In this way, they could make a sharp cutting tool. Stone tools were sometimes tied to a wooden handle.

These people are using different tools. One woman is cutting animal skins to make clothes. Another woman is punching holes in a piece of skin. The man is tying a sharp stone to a stick to make a spear.

Early people used flint to make their tools. They dug deep into the ground to find chunks of hard flint. They broke flint into flakes that had sharp edges.

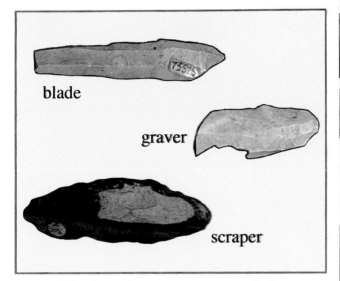

The blade above was used for carving. The graver made holes in leather. The scraper was used to clean leather.

The first metal used by people was copper. Above is a copper ax head. Later, people used bronze, a harder metal made from copper and tin.

People used wood, deer antlers, or stone to make flint tools.

First they shaped the flint roughly by striking it.

Then they chipped away sides of the flint to sharpen it.

This flint blade was used as a knife or spear head.

The first pottery

More than 8,000 years ago people made pots for cooking and holding food. They dug clay out of the ground to make pots. The pots were baked in a fire to make the clay hard. The first pots were plain. Later, people decorated their pots.

This woman is digging up clay with a wooden tool. She uses her hands to squeeze the lumps of clay into balls.

The woman rolls each ball of clay between her hands to form a long clay stick. The clay is mixed with water to keep it soft and easy to handle.

To form a pot, the woman coils the clay stick around and around. One clay stick makes a small pot. Larger pots need two or more sticks of clay.

4

Next, the woman smooths the coils of clay into the right shape for a pot.

5

Now the pot must be baked hard in a fire. After the clay is hard, the pot is left to cool.

This pot was found in Egypt. A pattern of animals was painted on it before the pot was baked.

The pattern of marks on this pot were made on the soft clay with a pointed stick.

The first clothes

The first people were hunters. They dressed in animal skins, like this Cro-Magnon man. In later times people became farmers. Farmers kept sheep for meat and wool. Wool was made into cloth. Wool clothing was softer and warmer.

The pictures below show how early people made clothes. They used animal skins.

First the skin was cleaned. Then it was stretched on the ground and left to dry.

The skin was then cut up. Holes were made along the edges. Pieces were sewn together with dried grass or leather strips.

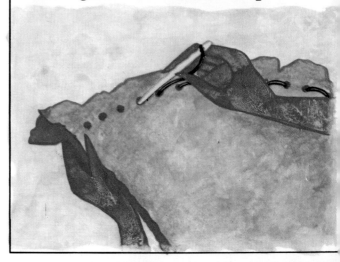

The Egyptians grew flax to make yarn. Then they wove the yarn on a loom to make linen.

loom

This Egyptian woman is using makeup on her eyes. Her mirror is made of polished bronze.

In Egypt, both men and women wore jewelry. Some of the jewelry was worn for good luck.

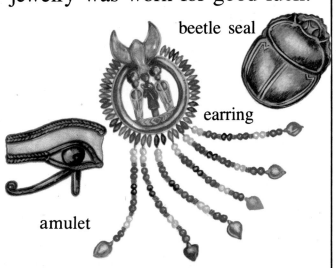

beetle seal

earring

amulet

This woman lived in Egypt more than 3,000 years ago. Because it was hot in Egypt, she wore light, loose clothes made of linen. She wore sandals on her feet. Her hair is decorated with beads. Rich women often wore gold or silver jewelry.

The first paintings

The Cro-Magnons were the first people we know about who painted pictures. They made pictures on cave walls of animals they hunted. They thought their pictures might bring them luck in the hunt.

Paint was made of powder from colored rock mixed with water or animal fat. Animal hair or sticks were used for brushes.

Sometimes people painted this way. They wet the cave wall. Then they blew colored powder at the wall through a tube.

The first writing

We know a lot about people of long ago from their writings. The Sumerians were the first people to use writing. They used picture signs. People in different parts of the world used different picture signs. The picture at the right shows some Egyptian writing.

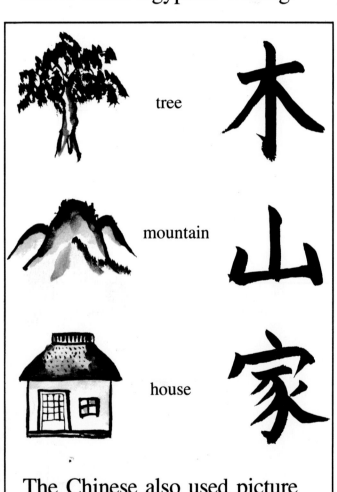

tree

mountain

house

The Chinese also used picture signs. Here are some Chinese picture signs and the things they stand for.

At first, the Chinese scratched or painted signs on bone or wood. Later they invented a kind of paper made from rags.

Sumerian picture signs later became wedge-shaped marks. Special tools were used to press the marks into clay.

In Roman times people wrote by scratching letters on wax-covered tablets. They used a pointed metal tool.

EARLY CIVILIZATIONS

The Sumerians

The Sumerians lived over 5,000 years ago. Their land was called Mesopotamia. They farmed the rich land between two rivers. One Sumerian city, called Ur, has been dug up. Many treasures were found.

The picture at the left shows how the Sumerians dressed.

The Sumerians built huge platforms. This one was built at Ur. At the top of the stairs was a temple.

This model of a goat in a bush was found at Ur. It is made of gold and precious stones.

Sumerian buildings were made of clay bricks. First, men mixed lumps of clay.

The clay was shaped into bricks. The bricks were left in the hot sun to bake hard.

Then the bricks were built up in rows. Sumerian brick buildings lasted a long time.

Egyptian kings were called pharaohs. When the pharaohs died, they were sometimes buried in pyramids with all their treasures. Thousands of workers were needed to build the pyramids.

Above is a statue of a sphinx. It has a lion's body and a human head. It was built to honor the sun god.

The Egyptians

The Nile River in Egypt flooded every year. This made the land around the river good for farming. The Egyptians began to farm this land over 6,000 years ago. They grew grains, fruit, and vegetables.

The Egyptians made special coffins for their kings and queens. This one is richly decorated.

The workers used ropes to drag the huge blocks of stone up the pyramids. In this picture, the builder is showing his plans.

The Minoans

The Minoans lived 4,500 years ago on the island of Crete. They were named after a legendary king called Minos. The Minoans were farmers and traders.

One old story said that King Minos kept a fierce beast called the Minotaur. A brave man called Theseus killed it.

The Minoan kings lived in a city called Knossos. The king had a beautiful palace. The queen had a bathroom with running water. You can see this palace today. Parts of it have been rebuilt to show what it looked like thousands of years ago.

The Minoans liked the sport of bull-leaping. Teams of young men and women would somersault over a bull's horns.

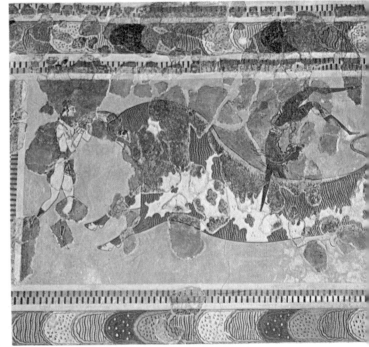

The Phoenicians were sailors and traders. They sailed as far as West Africa to trade.

The Phoenicians

The Phoenicians lived along the east Mediterranean coast. They were clever shipbuilders and brave sailors. They sailed across the Mediterranean and built cities like Carthage in North Africa.

The Phoenicians were skilled at crafts. They carved ivory figures like this one. They also made colored glass ornaments.

The Hittites

For a long time people made tools and weapons from copper and bronze. The Hittites were among the first to use iron. Iron is much stronger than bronze.

The Hittites ruled a large empire for over 200 years. They used iron weapons like those at the right.

Hittite blacksmiths were important men. They made iron tools and weapons.

The Indus River cities

Even 4,000 years ago some cities were like our cities today. Mohenjo-daro, a city by the Indus River, had brick buildings. Houses had bathrooms. Water ran through clay pipes from a tank on the roof.

A great bath has been found at Mohenjo-daro. It may have been used by the priests.

The Indus people worshipped many gods and goddesses. Above is a statue of an Indus goddess.

This cart is carrying straw. Straw was used for making the roofs of houses. Oxen were used to pull carts like this.

The Yellow River settlements

People in China, like those in Egypt and Mesopotamia, settled near a large river. Chinese people settled near the Yellow River, or Hwang-Ho, 7,000 years ago. In addition to farming, the Chinese became skilled craft workers.

The Chinese made beautiful statues of clay, bronze, and jade. This dragon is bronze.

The Chinese grew rice near the Yellow River. They dug canals to bring water from the river to their rice fields.

The Chinese used bronze to
make weapons, tools, pots, and
statues. Bronze is made by
melting copper and tin together.
These men are pouring the
melted metal into a mold.

The Assyrians

The Assyrians lived in the Middle East, near the valley of the Tigris River. The Assyrians were traders. Sometimes they were attacked as they carried goods to other lands. So they became skilled soldiers and fought many battles.

The Assyrians invented many war machines. This machine could break down city walls.

Above is a great Assyrian king killing a lion. Lions had to be hunted because they killed cows and sheep.

Assyrians used bows and arrows tipped with iron. In battle, soldiers hid behind shields of woven twigs. The shields could be moved about.

The Babylonians

Babylon was a great city built on the banks of the Euphrates River. One of its famous rulers was King Nebuchadnezzar II. More than 2,500 years ago, he had magnificent monuments and temples built in Babylon. There was a huge temple there known to us as the Tower of Babel.

royal
hunter

Ishtar Gate

The Ishtar Gate, which you can see here, was one of the twelve gates that led into the city of Babylon. The gate is decorated with carvings of dragons and bulls. It was built in honor of the god Marduk.

The Greeks had many gods.
Zeus was their chief god.

Athene, goddess of wisdom,
had her main temples in Athens.

The Greeks

The Greeks lived in southeast
Europe over 2,000 years ago.
They built Sparta, Athens, and
other famous cities. Sometimes
one man ruled a city. Sometimes
many men were in control.

The Greeks were famous for
their artists. This is a head of
Aphrodite, the goddess of love.

Apollo, the sun god, was a handsome son of Zeus.

Artemis, goddess of hunting, was another daughter of Zeus.

In Greece, games were held in Olympia every four years. On the left is a scene from one of these first Olympic games.

The Greeks made beautiful vases. This one shows a scene from a Greek story.

The Seven Wonders of the World

About 2,000 years ago, a Greek writer made a list of famous statues and buildings. They were called the Seven Wonders of the World. All except one of them have been destroyed or have fallen into ruins. Only the pyramids of Egypt remain today.

At the right is the Colossus of Rhodes, a huge statue of the Greek god Apollo. It stood by the harbor of Rhodes. An earthquake destroyed it.

Above are some of the pyramids of Egypt. The pyramids were royal tombs. They had rooms and passages inside.

Mausolus was a king in Asia Minor. When he died, his wife built him a huge tomb. It was called the Mausoleum.

The Greeks built this temple at Ephesus to honor their goddess of hunting, Artemis. After many years, the temple was destroyed by an attacking army.

This huge lighthouse was called the Pharos. It was built in Egypt by the Greeks.

King Nebuchadnezzar built the Hanging Gardens of Babylon, shown above. Water was pumped from the ground up to the high gardens.

Below is a statue of the Greek god Zeus. It was made of marble, ivory, and gold. It stood at Olympia in Greece.

THE ROMAN WORLD

The first Romans were farmers and warriors. They spread Roman rule through Italy about 300 years before Christ. Later, the Roman emperors ruled half of Europe. They also ruled parts of Africa and Asia.

The Romans built large arenas like this one. People came there to watch games.

Rome had the best trained army in the world. The army was divided into groups called legions. There were about 6,000 men in each legion. Most soldiers fought on foot with short swords or spears. A few soldiers rode horses.

Roman soldiers built forts and roads in the lands they fought in. You can see the remains of many Roman buildings today.

In a Roman city

A Roman city called Pompeii was buried under ash when a volcano blew up. Many years later the city was dug from the ashes. Some buildings were unharmed. Pompeii can show us how the Romans lived. You can still see homes, palaces, and Roman art there.

When Pompeii was dug up, many Roman bodies were found covered in hard ash.

Rich people in Pompeii had fine furniture. Rooms were heated by pipes under the floors.

This house was only partly hurt by the volcano. Its wall paintings are almost as good as new.

At the left is a street in Pompeii. You can see the many old buildings. It must have been terrifying when the hot ash rained down on the city.

Some Celts built villages on hill tops. In this picture they are fighting Romans.

The Celts

The Celts conquered much of Europe. They were fierce fighters but were defeated by the Romans except in Scotland and Ireland.

The Celtic chiefs and their wives often wore gold bands called torques.

Today, Celtic people live in Wales, Scotland, Ireland, Cornwall, and Brittany.

Saxon nobles held feasts in great halls like this. They liked to hear songs about Saxon heroes.

The Saxons

The Saxons came from northern Europe. They invaded Britain after the Romans left. They set up kingdoms in England and farmed the land. One great Saxon king was Alfred the Great. Alfred fought the Danes when they attacked Britain.

One Saxon king was buried in his ship. This purse clasp was found buried with him.

The sack of Rome

Rome was a powerful city for more than 1,000 years. Then, in the year 410, an enemy army of Visigoths invaded Italy. Alaric was the leader of the Visigoths. He said he would destroy Rome if the Romans did not give him money. They refused.

The Visigoths broke down the city gates. They burned buildings, stole treasures, and killed many Romans. This was called the sack of Rome.

NEW EMPIRES

Byzantium

Diocletian was Emperor of Rome from the years 284 to 305. He felt that the empire was too big to be ruled from one place. He divided it into two parts. One part was ruled from Rome. The other part was ruled from Byzantium.

Byzantine churches were decorated with mosaic pictures. Mosaics were made of many small pieces of colored stone.

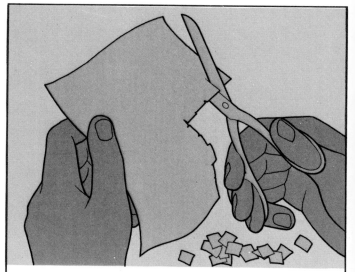

You can make your own mosaic pictures. First, cut out tiny squares of colored paper. Use several different colors.

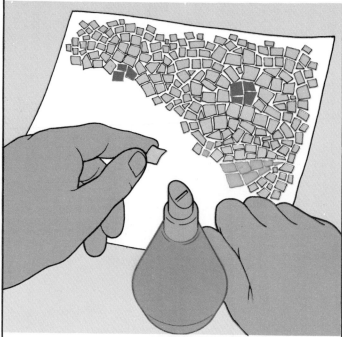

Next, use the colored squares to make a pattern or picture. Use paste or glue to stick the squares to a plain white sheet.

The capital of the Byzantine
Empire was named
Constantinople after the emperor
Constantine. It became a
crowded, busy, and
important city.

The rise of Islam

Muhammad was an Arab who lived in Mecca. After the year 610, he started a new religion called Islam. Today, Islam is the faith of most Arabs and many Africans and Asians. Mecca became the holy city of Muhammad's followers, who are called Muslims.

The Muslims built great cities such as Baghdad in Iraq and Cairo in Egypt. They worshipped in temples called mosques.

Muslim armies conquered a great empire. They often used camels as well as horses when they fought in the desert.

The Vikings

The Vikings came by sea from Scandinavia. They invaded Britain and western Europe in the 800s. They burned down houses and stole treasures. Later, they began to settle in the lands they had raided. They became farmers. They built villages.

The Vikings were great sailors. Their ships reached Greenland, Iceland, and North America.

The carved dragon's head on the left is from a Viking ship. The Vikings decorated their ships with heads like this. They made wide-bodied ships for trading and long, narrow ships for fighting.

Some Viking chiefs were buried in their ships. Some of these ships have been found. This one was found buried in Norway.

A single oar with a wide blade was fixed at the back of the ship. It was used for steering.

HIC EXEVNT: CABALL

The Normans

Vikings who settled in France were called Normans. A Norman leader called William believed that England should belong to him. The English wanted their own king, Harold. William led an army of Normans to England. He defeated Harold and became king of England. He was called William the Conqueror.

The Normans built castles like this one to guard their lands.

turrets

chapel

main entrance

well

DAN ESCOTT

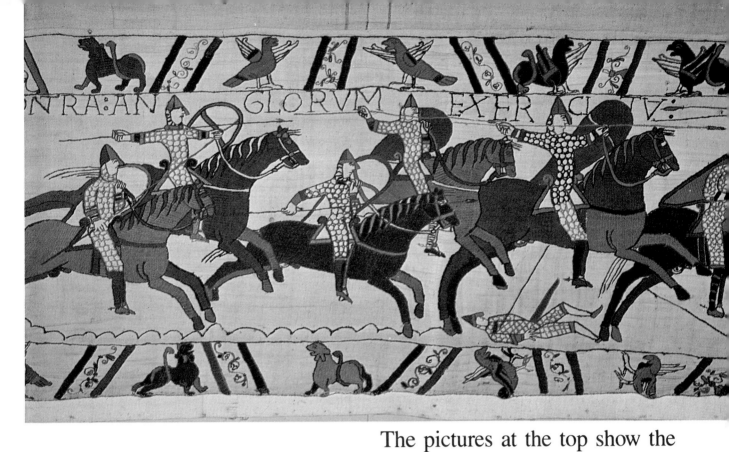

The pictures at the top show the Norman Conquest of England in 1066. At the left are Norman ships sailing to England. Above are some Norman knights.

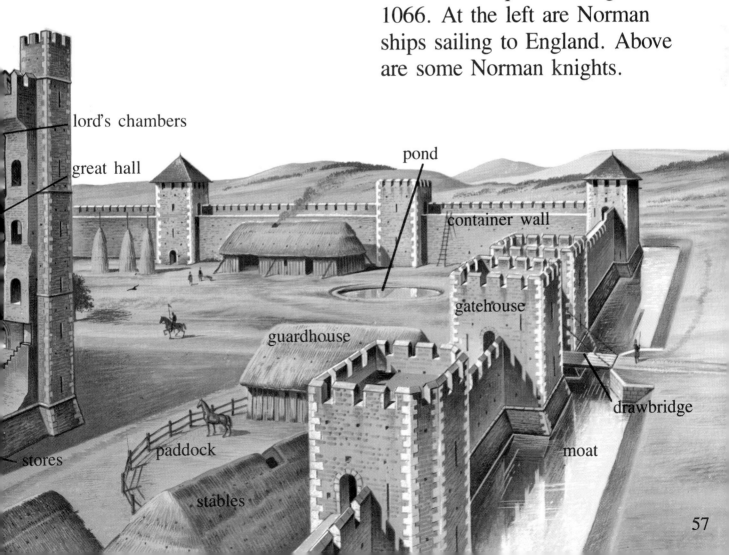

lord's chambers

great hall

pond

container wall

gatehouse

guardhouse

drawbridge

stores

paddock

moat

stables

The Great Wall of China is thousands of kilometers long. It was built to keep out invaders.

The Chinese

The Yellow River settlements grew into the huge country of China. China was ruled by an emperor. The emperor was believed to be a god. Anyone who did not obey him was punished. Most Chinese were poor farmers. They worked very hard.

Chinese craft workers made jade figures like this horse.

The Chinese invented many new things. They used gunpowder to make fireworks.

The Chinese invented a simple compass about 2,000 years ago. It was not used anywhere else for a thousand years.

The Chinese invented printing. The printer pressed a sheet of paper on inked picture signs carved into blocks of wood.

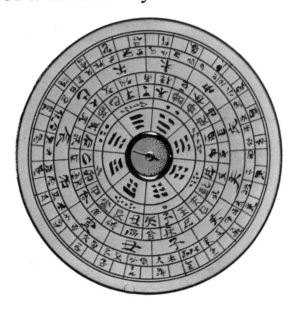

The Japanese

Japan is made up of several islands. In stone age times hunters and fishers lived on these islands. The first emperor was Jimmu. It is believed he ruled 600 years before the time of Christ.

Samurai warriors ruled Japan for over 600 years. They were brave soldiers. Their armor was made from hundreds of iron links. It protected them from arrows.

The Japanese made houses of bamboo. They relaxed in their beautiful gardens of sand, rocks, and trees.

On the left, some Japanese ladies are serving tea. This is how they welcomed guests.

The Maya

The Maya lived a thousand years ago in Central America. Their farmers grew corn. The Maya built great pyramids.

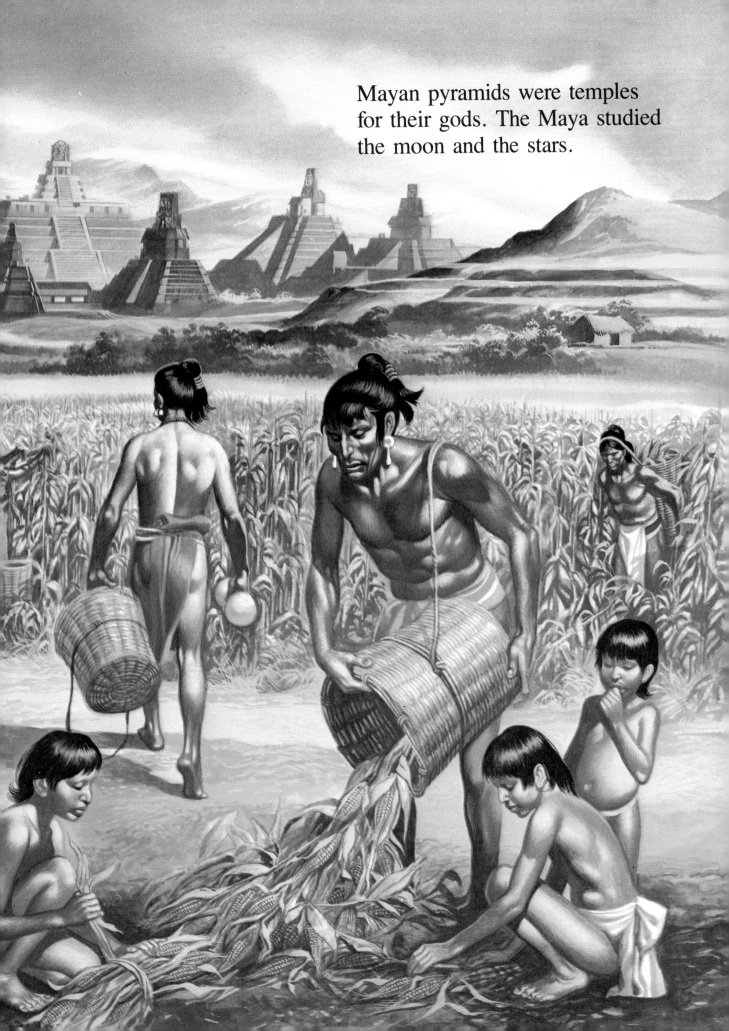

Mayan pyramids were temples
for their gods. The Maya studied
the moon and the stars.

GLOSSARY

These words are defined the way they are used in the book.

antler (ANT luhr) the horn of an animal in the deer family

Aphrodite (AF ruh DYT ee) the Greek goddess of love

Apollo (uh PAHL oh) the Greek god of sunlight and music

arrow (AIR oh) a thin weapon with a pointed head that is shot from a bow

Artemis (ART uh muhs) the Greek goddess of the hunt

Assyrian (us SIHR ee uhn) a person who lived in the ancient country of Assyria

Babylon (BAB uh lahn) an ancient city in the country of Babylonia

bamboo (bam BOO) a woody grass with hollow stems used for building

blacksmith (BLAK smihth) a person who makes things from iron

bronze (brahnz) a metal that is made of copper and tin

Byzantium (bih ZAN tee uhm) an ancient city of eastern Europe

Celt (sehlt) someone who belonged to an early tribe of western Europe

Chinese (chy NEEZ) people who live in the country of China

compass (KUHM puhs) a small machine that shows directions such as north or south

Constantinople (kahn stan tih NOH puhl) a large city of eastern Europe; it was formerly called Byzantium

copper (KAHP uhr) a common soft red metal

cotton (KAHT uhn) a soft cloth made from plants

Crete (kreet) an island belonging to Greece, in the Mediterranean sea

Cro-Magnon (kroh MAG nuhn) an ancient group of people

decorate (DEHK uh rayt) to cover something with pretty patterns or jewelry

discover (dihs KUHV uhr) to find something that had not been seen or known before

earthquake (UHRTH kwayk) a shaking of the ground that can hurt buildings and people

Egyptian (ih JIHP shuhn) someone who lives in the middle eastern country of Egypt

emperor (EHM puhr uhr) a person who rules over many lands and people

fireworks (FYR wuhrks) things that can make bright explosions in the sky

flax (flaks) a plant that can be used to make cloth

flint (flihnt) a hard rock that can be made into sharp objects

frame (fraym) something that is made from many parts put together

furniture (FUHR nih chuhr) objects such as tables and chairs that are used in a house

grain (grayn) a kind of plant that can be used for food

graver (GRAY vuhr) a sharp tool used to cut things

groove (groov) a long narrow cut in something

gunpowder (GUHN poud uhr) different powders put together that explode

Hittite (HIH tyt) someone who belonged to an ancient people of western Asia

Indus (IHN duhs) a river that flows through what is now Pakistan, India, and China

invade (ihn VAYD) to enter a place in order to take it over

invent (ihn VEHNT) to think up something for the first time

iron (eyern) a heavy metal

Islam (ihs LAHM) a religion based on the belief in Allah as God and Muhammed as his prophet

jade (jayd) a shiny green stone

jewelry (JOO uhl ree) objects such as rings or necklaces worn on the body

knight (nyt) a fighting man of the Middle Ages who rode a horse

Knossos (NAHS uhs) a great city of ancient Crete

leather (LEH thuhr) a tough substance made of animal skin

legion (LEE juhn) the main unit of the Roman army, having 3000 to 6000 men

lighthouse (LYT hous) a tall building with a strong light to guide ships

Mediterranean (MEHD uh tuh *RAY* nee uhn) a sea between Europe and Africa

Mesopotamia (MEHS uh puh *TAY* mee uh) an ancient land in southwest Asia

Minoan (muh NOH uhn) belonging to ancient Crete

Minotaur (MIHN uh tawr) a monster that is half man, half bull

mosaic (moh ZAY ihk) a picture made from small pieces of colored material

mosque (mahsk) a building used for worship by Muslims

Nebuchadnezzar (NEHB uh kuhd NEHZ uhr) an ancient king of Babylon

Norman (NAWR muhn) belonging

to a French people who conquered England in 1066

ornament (AWR nuh muhnt) something that adds beauty

pharaoh (FEHR oh) a ruler of ancient Egypt

Phoenician (fih NEE shuhn) a person who lived in the ancient country of Phoenicia in southwest Asia

precious (PREHSH uhs) full of worth

printing (PRIHNT ihng) the practice of making printed letters on a page with a machine

pyramid (PIHR uh mihd) an ancient building with a square base and four triangular walls

Roman (ROH muhn) a person who lived in the empire of ancient Rome

samurai (SAM uh ry) a Japanese soldier of the past

Scandinavia (skan duh NAY vee uh) an area in northern Europe that contains the countries Norway and Sweden

somersault (SUHM uhr sault) the act of rolling head over heels and landing on your feet

Sphinx (sfings) a huge Egyptian statue with the body of a lion and the head of a human

statue (STACH oo) a solid figure

of a person or animal that is often cut out of stone

Sumerian (soo MEHR ee uhn) a person who lived in the ancient country of Sumer, a south part of Babylonia

tomb (toom) a building where dead people are buried

torque (tawrk) a metal collar worn by ancient Celts

vegetable (VEHJ tuh buhl) food that comes from plants

village (VIHL ihj) a group of homes; smaller than a town

Visigoth (VIHZ uh gahth) a person who belongs to an ancient people who invaded Rome

volcano (vahl KAY noh) a hole in the earth's crust that lets out hot steam and melted rock

wedge (wehj) a shape like a triangle that is wide at one end and pointed at the other

worship (WUHR shuhp) prayer and other acts done in honor of God

writing (RYT ihng) to make letters on a surface

Zeus (zoos) the Greek god who is king of the gods

FURTHER READING

Asimov, Isaac. *The Egyptians*. Boston: Houghton, Mifflin, 1967. 256pp.

Beck, Barbara L. *The Ancient Maya.* New York: F. Watts, 1983.

Cottrell, Leonard. *The Mystery of Minoan Civilization.* New York: World Pub., Co., 1971. 128pp.

Duggan, Alfred L. *The Romans.* Cleveland: World Pub. Co., 1964. 125pp.

Edmonds, I. G. *Islam.* New York: F. Watts, 1977. 65pp.

Ellacott, Samuel E. *The Norman Invasion.* New York: Abelard-Schuman, 1966. 160pp.

Fagg, Christopher. *Ancient Greece.* New York: Warwick Press, 1978. 44pp.

Fagg, Christopher. *Lost Cities.* Windermere, Florida: Rourke, 1981.

Field, Gordan. *The Minoans of Ancient Crete.* New York: Crowell, 1964. 100pp.

Garber, Janet, ed. *The Concise Encyclopedia of Ancient Civilizations.* New York: F. Watts, 1978.

Goode, Ruth. *People of the First Cities.* New York: Macmillan, 1977.

Greenberg, Lorna. *The Aztecs.* New York: F. Watts, 1983.

Greene, Carla. *Man and Ancient Civilization.* Indianapolis: Bobbs-Merrill Co., Inc., 1977.

Hamey, J. A. *The Roman Engineers.* Minneapolis: Lerner Publishing, 1982.

Horton, Casey. *Ancient Greeks.* New York: Gloucester Press, 1984.

Jones, John Ellis. *Ancient Greece.* New York: Warwick Press, 1983.

Leonard, Jonathan N. *Early Japan*. New York: Time-Life Books, 1968. 191pp.

Marcus, Rebecca B. *Prehistoric Cave Paintings*. New York: F. Watts, 1968. 88pp.

Maynard, Christopher. *Prehistoric Life*. New York: Warwick Press, 1976. 48pp.

Millard, Anne. *Ancient Egypt*. New York: Warwick Press, 1979. 44pp.

Millard, Anne. *Early People*. New York: Warwick Press, 1982.

Purdy, Susan. *Ancient Egypt*. New York: F. Watts, 1982.

Robinson, Charles Alexander. *Ancient Greece*. New York: F. Watts, 1984.

Robinson, Charles Alexander. *The First Book of Ancient Egypt*. New York: F. Watts, 1961. 61pp.

Rosalie, David. *Ancient Egypt*. New York: Warwick Press, 1984.

Scott, Joseph and Lenore Scott. *Egyptian Hieroglyph for Everyone*. New York: Funk and Wagnalls, 1968. 95pp.

Sheehan, Angela, ed. *The Prehistoric World*. New York: Warwick Press, 1976. 160pp.

Starr, Chester G. *Early Man: Prehistory and the Civilizations of the Ancient Near East*. New York: Oxford University Press, 1973. 206pp.

Suskind, Richard. *The Sword of the Prophet: the Story of the Moslem Empire*. New York: Grosset and Dunlap, 1972. 90pp.

Thwaite, Anthony. *Beyond the Inhabited World: Roman Britain*. New York: Seabury Press, 1976. 125pp.

Unstead, R. J. *Looking at Ancient History*. New

York: Macmillan Company, 1960. 112pp.

Walker, Richard L. *Ancient China and Its Influence in Modern Times*. New York: F. Watts, 1969. 86pp.

World Book-Childcraft International, Inc. *The World Book Encyclopedia*. 22 volumes. Chicago: World Book-Childcraft International, Inc., 1980.

QUESTIONS TO THINK ABOUT

The First Men and Women

Do you remember?

How do we know what early people looked like?

How did the earliest people get food? How did later people get food?

How did people feel when they first saw fire?

What did the Cro-Magnon people live in?

Find out about . . .

Cro-Magnon people. Where did they live? How tall were they? What kinds of tools did they use?

Fire. Why was the discovery of fire important? How did fire help early people? What are some ways to make fire without matches?

Early houses. Why are houses important? How do they help people? What did early people use to make houses?

Early farmers. Some early farmers lived near the Danube River in Europe. What kind of houses did they build? What crops did they grow? What did a Danubian village look like?

Crafts and Tools

Do you remember?

What were the first tools made from?

What was the first metal people made? What metal did they make later?

How did early hunters dress? What did farmers use to make clothes?

What kind of pictures did Cro-Magnons paint? Where did they paint them?

Who were the first people to use writing?

Find out about . . .

Early tools. How do we know about early tools? What kind of tools have been found?

Pottery. What did early people use pots for? Why is clay good for making pots? How did pottery change over the years?

Cave paintings. Where have cave paintings been found? What is shown on these early cave paintings?

Writing. What early people used picture signs for writing? How did picture signs change over a long time? Who were the first people to use an alphabet? Where does our alphabet come from?

Early Civilizations

Do you remember?

What is Ur?

What were the pyramids used for? What is the sphinx?

Where did the Minoans live? Where did the Phoenicians live?

Who were the first people to use iron?

Where was Mohenjo-daro? In what ways was it like a city today?

What people lived along the Yellow River?

What were the Assyrians known for? What city did they destroy?

Who invented the Olympic games?

Which of the Seven Wonders of the World can be seen today?

Find out about . . .

The Fertile crescent. What was the Fertile Crescent? What early people lived there?

Pyramids. When were the pyramids built? How big were they? When did people first learn about the tombs inside them? What was found in the tomb of King Tut?

The Hebrew people. Who were the Hebrew people? Where did they live? What other early people lived near them? How did the Hebrews differ from other groups of people?

The Minotaur. What was the Minotaur? What is the story about Theseus and the Minotaur?

Greek gods. Who were some of the Greek gods? What are some of the stories about them?

The Trojan War. What was the Trojan War? Who fought it? Who wrote a famous story about it? What is the story called? According to the story, how did the war start? How long did it last? How did it end?

Famous Greeks. Here are some famous Greeks: Pericles, Sappho, Hippocrates, Phidias, Socrates, Alexander the Great. Find out more about some of these people.

The Roman World

Do you remember?

What were the Roman legions?

What things did Roman soldiers build?

What Roman city was buried under ashes? What happened to the buildings in this city?

Where did the Celts live? Who did they fight? Who won?

What was the Sack of Rome? When did it happen?

Find out about . . .

Julius Caesar. Who was Julius Caesar? What did he do for Rome?

Pompeii. What volcano blew up near the city? When did it happen? When was the city dug up again? What was found there?

Visigoths. Who were the Visigoths? Where did they come from? What lands did they conquer?

Alfred the Great. When did King Alfred rule in England? Why was he called "the Great"?

New Empires

Do you remember?

Who was Diocletian? Who was Constantine?

What city was the capital of Byzantium?

What are mosaics?

When did Islam begin? Who started this religion? Where did it spread to?

What cities did the Muslims build? What are mosques?

Where did the Vikings come from? When did they invade England?

Who were the Normans?

Who fought in the battle of Hastings? Why did they fight? Who won?

What are some Chinese inventions?

Who was Genghis Khan? What lands did he conquer?

How did the Japanese welcome guests?

Who were the Samurai?

Where did the Maya live? What did they build?

Find out about . . .

Byzantium. Where was Byzantium? How long

did the empire last? Where is Constantinople? What is that city called today?

The Crusades. What were the Crusades? Who fought in them? Why?

Viking sailors. Who was Eric the Red? Who was Leif Ericsson? What did Eric discover? What did Leif discover?

Norman castles. Why did the Normans build castles? What was life like in a castle? Are any of these castles still standing today?

The Great Wall. Why was the Great Wall of China built? How long did it take to build it?

Aztecs and Incas. Who were the Aztecs? Who were the Incas? Where did these people live? What were their cities like?

Civilizations in North America. Who were the first people to live in North America? Who were the Pueblos? What kind of houses did they build? Who were the Mound Builders? Why did they build mounds?

PROJECTS

Project — A Museum Trip

Museums have tools, clothing, and many other things that were used by people of long ago. Find out about museums in your area. Plan a trip to a museum. Look for things left behind by people you read about in this book.

Project — Ancient Civilizations

Choose at least six different early civilizations or empires. Find pictures that show something in each one. Cut the pictures from old magazines or draw them yourself.

Next, get a large poster board and a small map of the world. Paste the map at the center of the poster board. Paste the pictures around the map.

Then get some colored yarn or string. Pin or tape the yarn so that it makes a straight line from a picture to a place on the map. Be sure each piece of yarn points to the right place on the map. A picture of pyramids, for example, should be connected to Egypt, where the pyramids were built. Use this book or other books to help you find the right places on the map.

INDEX

Photo Credits: British Museum; Werner Form Archive; French Government Tourist Office; Michael Holford; Picturepoint Ltd.; Staatliches Museum, Berlin.

Front cover: Grant Heilman.

Illustrators: Jim Bamber; Roger Phillips; John Bilham; Peter Robinson; Jeffrey Burns; Chris Simmons; Dick Eastland; Andrew Skilleter; John Fraser; Raymond Turvey; Elizabeth Graham-Yool; Colin Hawkins; Ron Haywood; Richard Hook; Illustra; Eric Jewell; Ben Manchipp; Peter North.